Original title:
The Oak's Odes

Copyright © 2025 Creative Arts Management OÜ
All rights reserved.

Author: Nash Everly
ISBN HARDBACK: 978-1-80566-675-2
ISBN PAPERBACK: 978-1-80566-960-9

Whispers of Ancient Bark

In a forest blushed with green,
Bark talks more than you have seen.
It tells of squirrels with grand schemes,
And birds who forget their sunny dreams.

Leaves giggle as they sway and swirl,
They gossip of acorns and a twirl.
The wind joins in with a whoosh and hum,
While mice play tag and share a crumb.

Canopy Dreams

Above the world where shadows play,
A raccoon dreams of a cabaret.
In acorn hats they dance and prance,
While crickets cheer in a wild trance.

The sun peeks through like a curious cat,
Watching critters in their fancy hat.
With every leap, a chuckle shared,
Who knew a squirrel could be so wildly dared?

Beneath the Gnarled Boughs

Beneath the branches, a party brews,
With chipmunks breaking all the news.
They laugh at clouds and bloated bugs,
While ants march on, all tight like hugs.

Gnarled roots play hide and seek, you see,
Telling tales so hilariously.
The mossy faces cheer them on,
As laughter echoes from dusk till dawn.

Roots in Reverie

Roots stretch deep with a quirky grin,
Whispering secrets of all they've seen.
They poke at critters and tease the ground,
"Oh look, a snail, and he's not around!"

They keep the stories of seasons lost,
Of raindrops, sunshine, and the frost.
With every wiggle, they pull a jest,
In this wooden world, they're truly blessed.

Songs of the Timeless Tree

In the breeze, a rustling sound,
Leaves gossip about the ground.
Squirrels dance with acorn hats,
Chasing shadows, dodging cats.

A branch dips low, a bird takes flight,
Worms throw parties every night.
With every sway, a joke is told,
Nature's laughter—never cold.

Shadows of the Forest Elder

Wise old trunk with bark so deep,
Holds secrets that it loves to keep.
Throw in a joke as the sun dips low,
The shadows chuckle—'Just go with the flow!'

Raccoons prance in the pale moonlight,
Sharing rumors of the owl's flight.
'Whooo's the best problem solver here?'
Said the tree with a chuckle, 'Definitely me, dear!'

A Symphony of Leaves

Leaves compose a harmonized tune,
Swirling circles under the moon.
Wind whips in, a sneaky guest,
Tickling branches; they laugh the best.

A jay drops in for a quick chat,
Poking fun at the old fat rat.
'Life's a dance, watch me perform!'
Chirps the bright sparrow, full of charm.

Chronicles of the Sturdy Sentinel

Once a sprout, now standing tall,
Covered in tales, the tree recalls.
Squirrels and bugs take notes to share,
'You won't believe the stuff that's rare!'

With every ring, a story grows,
Of grooves and bumps, the gossip flows.
Who knew that time could be so fun?
Laughter echoes; the day is won!

The Language of Gnarled Limbs

With branches stretched, a giant waves,
Whispers travel through leafy caves.
Knots and twists, each story shared,
Squirrels gossip, all unprepared.

A crow once claimed, 'I'm the tree's muse!'
But owls hoot back, 'You just amuse!'
Rubber ducks in rainy pools,
Nature's laughter: one of its jewels.

Embracing the Sky's Canvas

Branches grasp at clouds above,
Like kids they leap, they dance and shove.
Colors splash in morning's light,
True artists playing, what a sight!

Leaves giggle as they flutter down,
While the breeze tickles the trunk's frown.
Butterflies prance in zig-zag lines,
Nature's clowns, with silly designs.

Lullabies of the Nature's Pillar

Nighttime wraps the gnarled limbs tight,
Crickets tune their songs of night.
In the shadows, creatures plot,
A party starts—if only the plot!

Fireflies blink like starlit fools,
While raccoons sneak, ignoring rules.
'What's for snacks?' a badger proclaims,
Nature's lullabies, with silly games.

The Heartbeat of the Green Realm

Roots stretch deep, they tickle the ground,
'Can you feel the pulse?' is the sound.
A worm drives by in a little car,
Singing loudly, 'I'm a tree's star!'

The grass chuckles at ants in a race,
While frogs leap high, claiming their space.
In this realm where laughter flows,
Every leaf knows how humor grows.

Legends in Leaf and Wood

In the forest's grand embrace,
Leaves conspire with a grin,
Whispers claim a squirrel's race,
Who knew he'd fit right in?

Beneath a gnarled old tree's shade,
A raccoon spins a tall tale,
Of how he danced and played,
Wearing shoes made of snail.

Fairy folk on branches swing,
Clapping paws and wings in cheer,
With every tune, the branches sing,
All creatures gather here.

So don't forget to take a look,
At legends lurking in the green,
For who'll write the perfect book,
About a tree so keen?

From Acorn to Majesty

Once a tiny acorn hunched,
With dreams of vast renown,
He squeaked, 'I'll be quite the bunch!'
While still stuck in the ground.

A lurking critter made a bet,
That he'd never grow so high,
But with rain, he started to sweat,
And shot up to kiss the sky.

Now he's towering and proud,
Telling tales of craziest heights,
From the whispers of the crowd,
And the fluttering birdy flights.

Yet at night he shakes with glee,
As the stars wink at his might,
Saying, 'Here's a hint for free,
Enjoy the thrill tonight!'

The Guardian's Lullaby

Gentle leaves hum a soft tune,
As twilight paints the sky,
A guardian whispers to the moon,
'Keep your watchful eye.'

Squirrels nestle and snuggle tight,
While owls hoot a sleepy rhyme,
Crickets play till the dawn's light,
In perfect woodland time.

Bats glide through the silver beams,
While branches sway in tune,
Each creature lost in bedtime dreams,
Dancing to the enchanting croon.

So drift away under this roof,
Nature's lullaby sings it's best,
For in this wild wooded woof,
Every being finds their rest.

Harmony in the Whispering Wind

Wind scrolls through the verdant trees,
Telling secrets of the day,
Tickling leaves with a subtle breeze,
While butterflies join the play.

Frogs croak rhymes from the old pond,
Chirping birds pipe in delight,
With whispers sweet and free, they bond,
In a joyous, feathered flight.

Rabbits bounce and join the band,
With a hop and a playful spin,
Together they make merry and grand,
In the wind's soft, joyful din.

So dance along with nature's charms,
Where smiles grow on leafy faces,
For in this realm of leafy arms,
Fun thrives in all the right places.

The Breath of the Silent Nature

In a forest where whispers play,
Leaves gossip secrets all day.
Squirrels dance, quite the show,
While shadows giggle, never slow.

The breeze is a playful tease,
Tickling branches, with such ease.
A frog croaks tales of delight,
As crickets join, under moonlight.

The daisies roll, in sweetly jest,
Claiming titles, who's the best?
And wise old trees chuckle near,
Their barky jokes we hold dear.

Down below, worms wiggle tight,
Unaware of the stars at night.
Nature's antics, are quite the spree,
In stillness, they giggle with glee.

A Psalm of Glorious Growth

Tiny seeds in the dirt,
Dreaming of growing, never hurt.
They stretch and yawn, oh what a sight,
Reaching for sunshine, feeling light.

A little sprout with a grand plan,
Starts to dance, oh yes, it can!
Popping up in the morning dew,
Singing songs, to greet the crew.

The daisies wink with petals bright,
As sunflowers stretch to the height.
Each petal flaps a merry tune,
While earthworms wiggle to the moon.

Roses pose with dazzling flair,
While thorns pretend to have no care.
In this garden of silly spree,
Nature's laughter is wild and free.

Embracing the Cycle of Life

Autumn leaves that twirl and spin,
Whispering laughter as they begin.
They race together, a joyful lot,
In swirling winds, they tie a knot.

Winter brings a chilly chill,
Snowflakes giggle, oh what a thrill!
They tumble down, a frosty cheer,
Creating castles far and near.

Spring bursts forth in hues so bright,
As flowers bloom, a vibrant sight.
Bees buzz with a comical hum,
While seeds burst forth, what fun awaits them!

Summer's sun brings playful heat,
Where critters dance, in nature's beat.
Each season twirls in funny steps,
As life spins round, with joyful reps.

The Storyteller of Seasons

There's a tree, with tales to tell,
Of windy days and likes that fell.
Each season shares a merry jest,
With branches swaying, it's quite the fest.

Squirrels scamper, with acorns gripped,
While owls blink, as stories are flipped.
Sunshine beams down with a wink,
While leaves nod, as if to think.

Buds burst forth, in playful glee,
As the bird sings, not one, but three.
With each rustle, the tree confides,
Nature's laughter, it never hides.

Under every twinkling star's glance,
The storytellers invite us to dance.
A symphony of fun unfolds,
In nature's arms, laughter beholds.

Echoes of the Woodland Heart

In the forest where squirrels race,
The rabbits hop, oh what a chase!
A fox in boots, a hat askew,
Says, "Hey, folks! Let's paint the view!"

Under the branches, shadows play,
A frog calls out, 'It's singalong day!'
The trees all sway, with laughter bright,
As acorns drop, a dancing sight.

The Age of Twisting Limbs

Twisted branches giggle loud,
As bushes plot to join the crowd.
A beetle dons a paper crown,
Declares, "I'm ruler of this town!"

The bees perform their buzzing cheer,
While ants form lines, they persevere.
A worm slides in, a wiggly king,
With leafy fans, he starts to sing!

Beneath the Oak's Embrace

A picnic spread upon the ground,
With chattering birds all around.
A raccoon steals a slice of cake,
Squealing out, "Oh, what a mistake!"

The woodland critters join the feast,
With every crumb, they laugh the least.
The sunbeams dance, a happy show,
While shadows giggle just below.

Treetop Musings

High above, where whispers bloom,
A parrot squawks, 'There's room, there's room!'
The squirrels dare to tightrope walk,
As owls tune up for midnight talk.

The wind blows tales from afar,
As branches sway like a music bar.
With playful jests, they weave the night,
In laughter's arms, all feels just right.

Secrets Beneath the Forest

In the shadowed grove, a squirrel struts,
He boasts of acorns in his little ruts.
The mushrooms giggle, sprouting in a line,
Whispering secrets about the tree's vast spine.

A raccoon in the night steals snacks with glee,
He claims he's royalty, can't you see?
With paws so nimble, he dances with flair,
While a shy deer watches from behind a lair.

Resilience in the Face of Storms

When storms come howling, the branches sway,
A wise old tree laughs, 'Oh, come what may!'
With roots so sturdy, he stands his ground,
While squirrels cling tight as the winds go 'round.

The rain comes pouring like a jolly prank,
A chipmunk swims by, saying, 'What a tank!'
He paddles through puddles, a grin on his face,
'This is more fun than a high speed chase!'

The Dance of Sunlight and Shade

In the lively green, a sunbeam prances,
Dodging the shadows with playful glances.
A rabbit hops in, trying to catch light,
While a snail, unbothered, takes its own flight.

The dappled floor sparkles in hues of gold,
While the ferns whisper, 'Our tales will be told!'
A dance of shadows, a cavalcade bright,
In the joyful ballet of day and night.

Fables from the Sylvan Realm

Once there was a crow, clever and sly,
Who claimed he could teach stars how to fly.
But with a crow's luck, he tripped on a branch,
Fell into a bush—oh, what a chance!

Then came a tortoise, wise and quite slow,
With tales of adventure and paths that he'd know.
He chuckled, 'Dear crow, you'll learn at your pace,
That flying's more fun when you're not in a race!'

Chronicles of Sun and Rain

When sunshine tickles leaves so bright,
The trees all giggle, what a sight!
Raindrops play tag on bark's embrace,
Splashes of joy in nature's grace.

Squirrels dance a wobbly jig,
While puddles boast of their own gig,
The clouds grumble, 'What's all this fuss?'
Nature's circus, coming to us!

Sun sneezes, and the raindrops cheer,
Frogs croak loudly, bringing good cheer.
Together they sing in joyful refrain,
A chorus of laughter through sun and rain.

So gather round, let's shout hooray,
For nature's quirks make a merry play.
With every twist of season's fate,
Life's a jest, and isn't it great?

The Keeper of Secrets

In the quiet wood, whispers float,
A tree guards tales like a grand old coat.
Rabbits giggle as they overhear,
A bear's last blush and a squirrel's cheer.

Branches croon of who stole the pie,
While owls wink, saying, 'Oh my!'
The breeze carries gossip, soft and sweet,
With acorns acting as tiny feats.

Roots entwined, a secreter's pact,
They laugh at time, a friendly act.
The wind, a messenger, swift and shifty,
Spreads tales like butter, thick and nifty.

So listen close when shadows dote,
For every twig holds a funny note.
Secrets wrapped in bark and bough,
In this snug nook, take a bow!

Shadows Stretching Eastward

As daylight blinks, and shadows tease,
Trees play hopscotch with the breeze.
Leaves flutter like they've lost the plot,
Bouncing around, in sun's hot spot.

From west to east, they stretch so wide,
Creeping slowly, almost a glide.
A squirrel strolls, thinks it's all a game,
Chasing daylight, oh what a fame!

Tickling the ground with their leafy tips,
Shadows wink with playful quips.
"Catch me if you can!" they seem to say,
As night falls, they dance away.

So when you're out and you see them play,
Know that laughter leads the way.
With every stretch and every turn,
Nature laughs, and we all learn!

The Life of a Sturdy Heart

A trunk so thick, it tells a tale,
Of breezes felt and storms that hail.
Branches dance like arms in glee,
While roots grip earth, strong as can be.

Bark wears wrinkles like a wise old sage,
Every notch speaks of a page.
Saplings watch with eyes so bright,
Learning laughter in day and night.

When winds come howling, a heart won't flinch,
It stands firm, not a single inch.
With a chuckle that shimmers like sun,
Life's sturdy heart knows how to run!

So raise a toast to the trees we see,
For their sturdy hearts set natures free.
In every sway, there's humor to find,
A reminder to cherish the joyful kind!

The Story of Every Ring

Once I heard a squirrel boast,
Of acorns stolen, he'd make toast.
He'd stack them high and sing a tune,
While filling up his nutty room.

Each ring reflects a silly tale,
Of windy days and a tiny snail.
Who raced a beetle down the bark,
And lost the bet—oh, what a lark!

These tales are whispered in the breeze,
Of creatures playing tag with trees.
With every ring, I hear their cheer,
A leafy laugh for all to hear!

So gather round, my friends so dear,
For every year, there's fun and cheer.
A history of pranks and fun,
In every ring, a laugh begun!

Where Shadows Cast Dreams

In dappled light, I saw a fox,
Trying on some silly socks.
He danced around, a sight to see,
While puddles giggled, 'Come and be!'

A shadow chased a playful hare,
Who twitched his nose without a care.
Together they spun in a whirl,
As nearby leaves began to twirl.

The sun peeked in with a sunny grin,
As shadows leaped and stretched their chin.
They threw a party on the ground,
With laughter booming all around!

So if you wander where shadows play,
You'll find the fun that won't decay.
Just join the dance and laugh along,
In shadowed realms, you can't go wrong!

Serenity on a Worn Path

Upon a path where laughter's bred,
I saw a chicken dance instead!
With feathers flying all around,
She spun in circles, quite unbound.

A frog jumped high, with great delight,
And tried to leap to reach the height.
But landed in a muddy spot,
And quacked, 'It's not what I had thought!'

Mice played tag beneath a root,
While a wise old turtle chewed his foot.
'Life's too short for solemn ways!'
He chuckled loud through sunny rays.

So walk the path where giggles grow,
With every step, let laughter flow.
For in this place, the best of life,
Is found in joy, without the strife!

Legacy of the Woodland Watcher

In every branch, there's quite a tale,
From sneaky thieves, to a windy gale.
The woodland watcher, wise and keen,
Has seen the fun that's evergreen!

He chuckles soft at critter fights,
Where chipmunks bicker 'bout their rights.
'Let's share the seeds!' the wise one shouts,
As all the animals prance about.

His gaze has spied both friendship's bloom,
And monkey shenanigans that loom.
He knows that all who roam this space,
Bring joy and laughter, just in case!

So cherish well this ancient tree,
For laughter's root runs deep, you see.
In every ring and leaf that turns,
Lives joyful wisdom the watcher earns!

Echoing through the Seasons

In spring, the branches sway with glee,
They tickle the skies, oh so free.
The squirrels dance in a sunny ray,
Chasing each other all through the day.

Summer arrives, with a sun so bold,
The leaves look shiny, and the stories unfold.
Bugs throw parties, and roots play the tunes,
While shadows stretch like lazy loons.

Autumn's laughter rustles the air,
As leaves fall down, it's quite the affair.
Acorns roll like sneaky spies,
While critters collect them with twinkling eyes.

Winter whispers with snowflakes around,
Branches wear white like a gown, oh so profound.
Trees share secrets in frostbitten tones,
While the world sleeps, curled on its thrones.

Chronicles of the Woodland Guardian

Once a gentle giant stood, wise and old,
He wore a bark coat, so brave and bold.
With a fuzzy beard made of mossy fluff,
He smiled at the critters, saying, 'That's enough!'

His friends, the birds, squawked tales galore,
Of mischief and fun, of legends and lore.
Why did the rabbit wear those bright red shoes?
'Because he was hopping to chase away blues!'

The hedgehogs giggled, racing in line,
While planting their decorations of sweet pine.
And the wise old tree just chuckled with pride,
As leaves shared laughter in breezy stride.

With every new season, his heart filled with cheer,
For nature's wonders and friendships were near.
His branches swayed, a jovial beat,
For the woodland guardian thought life was a treat.

Reverie of the Leafy Canopy

Under the canopy, where shadows play,
Lies a world of fun, come join the fray.
The leaves whisper jokes as the breeze goes by,
While a cheerful raccoon gives a wink and a sigh.

'Why did the branch break up with the twig?'
Because it found someone with a bit more gig!
The laughter echoes through the boughs so bright,
As the sunlight dapples, a magical sight.

Bumblebees buzzing, creating a buzz,
Making sweet honey with all of the fuzz.
A dance of the petals, so bold and free,
Entwined with the laughter of a friendly bee!

As day turns to night and stars twinkle bright,
The leaves tell tales in soft moonlight.
With every rustle, a new joke is spun,
Under this canopy, life's just such fun!

Timelessness of the Whispering Trees

In a forest where time likes to play,
The trees chuckle softly in their own way.
'How long has it been since we all met here?'
'Forever, it seems, let's give a great cheer!'

One tree, named Charlie, with a twist in his bark,
Tells tales of the creatures that roam after dark.
'Why did the owl take a bath in the rain?'
'To make all his feathers as light as a plane!'

The willows dance with a graceful sway,
Inviting the wind to come join the play.
While the pines shout jokes of their needlepoint views,
About the squirrels' antics and bright-colored shoes.

As the seasons unfold, laughter remains,
Within every ring, joy runs through their veins.
These whispering trees, with their stories so fine,
Celebrate timelessness over sips of sunshine.

Nature's Pillar of Strength

In the forest stands a tree,
Wearing acorns like a hat.
It laughs with all its branches,
As squirrels skitter and chat.

A beetle tries to climb so high,
But slips and lands with a thud.
The tree just shakes with laughter,
Its trunk feels like a big hug.

Birds settle for a quick gossip,
While leaves dance in playful sways.
Nature's pillar, full of humor,
Keeps silly thoughts in sunny rays.

When the sun sets with a grin,
The tree winks and sighs out loud.
It knows every quirky tale,
A jester standing tall and proud.

Murmurs of the Mossy Floor

Beneath the giants, soft and green,
Moss cushions every footstep made.
Whispers tickle tiny toes,
As critters waltz in the shade.

A snail slides by, oh so slow,
With a shell like a stubborn car.
Moss remarks, 'I'll beat you home!'
As they chase the evening star.

Frogs croak out a ribbit cheer,
As worms wiggle with delight.
Moss giggles, 'This is my stage!'
Underneath the moonlight bright.

Each step on this blanket soft,
Is a tickle, a tease, a jest.
The floor of nature's funny play,
Where every creature feels blessed.

Dance of the Wind-Kissed Canopy

The leaves twist and twirl up high,
A ballroom where the breezes blow.
They giggle as they sway and swirl,
In nature's rhythm, they put on a show.

A cheeky gust whispers a joke,
While branches bend and laugh out loud.
'Catch me if you can!' they tease,
As they play with every cloud.

Birds flap wings, joining the fun,
Each chirp a note in the symphony.
The canopy sings a cheerful tune,
In a dance of wild harmony.

As twilight dips in rosy hues,
The leaves settle for a snooze.
Tomorrow's laughter will return,
In the canopy where the joy   brews.

Portrait of Resilience

A tree's gnarled face tells stories,
Of storms that tried to take its crown.
Yet here it stands, with a wink,
Wearing weather like a gown.

Its roots dig deep for laughs and cheer,
While branches rise to shake the sky.
With each lost leaf, it grins and says,
'I'll grow again, just watch me try!'

A raccoon knocks on its bark for food,
Yells, 'Hey, you've got great wisdom to share!'
The tree chuckles, 'Just have some patience,
And wait for the mane to repair!'

Through seasons harsh and summers wet,
This portrait smiles, wears strength like sheen.
In every ring, a tale is spun,
Of resilience and humor bright and keen.

Shadows of Wisdom

In the forest, I must say,
Wisdom wears a leafy cloak.
Squirrels argue, loud and gay,
While branches chuckle, 'What a joke!'

Rabbits hop with sage advice,
While owls wink, they know it all.
'Let's roll the dice, isn't life nice?'
Their laughter hangs, a playful call.

Clouds drift in, a shadowy crew,
Whispering secrets to the ground.
Beneath the boughs, the humor grew,
Trees shake with laughter all around.

Time dances on, with each soft breeze,
Reminding us not to be so grim.
Nature chuckles, it sure can tease,
In every shadow, joy's not slim.

The Dance of Autumn's Gait

Leaves pirouette, in gold and red,
A swirling ballet, no one will miss.
Squirrels leap like they've lost their head,
Chasing acorns, oh, the bliss!

With every crunch beneath our feet,
Laughter rises, a crisp delight.
A breeze carries whispers, oh so sweet,
As nature twirls in the fading light.

Frolicking fungi join the fun,
Like tiny dancers on the ground.
In autumn's glow, we've just begun,
To revel in joy all around.

So join the waltz, sway left and right,
With playful pumpkins, we shall gleam.
In this dance of sheer delight,
We find the joy behind the dream.

Roots Deep in Solitude

Down below where roots entwine,
A raucous party brews unseen.
Worms wear hats and dance in line,
While moles croon softly, quite serene.

They chat of soil, the tattle-tale,
With secrets deep, and tales of yore.
Underneath the leafy veil,
They laugh about life and what's in store.

With every twist, they break from strife,
As beetles tap their tiny toes.
Roots weave stories, much like life,
In solitude, the laughter grows.

So next you walk, just look below,
Where life's quirks bubble up to play.
In hidden depths, the giggles flow,
Roots know fun in their own way.

Harmonies of the Forest Floor

Underneath the lofty trees,
A symphony plays, soft and sweet.
Mossy carpets sway with ease,
While critters tap dance with their feet.

A chorus of chirps and gentle sighs,
Frogs croak along with a silly grin.
The forest floor, where laughter lies,
Nature's stage, the joy begins.

With every rustle, a note is struck,
As butterflies flutter, unaware.
In a concert of whimsy, who would've guessed,
The fawns are soloists beyond compare!

So lean in close, hear nature's jam,
A melody that's pure delight.
In the forest, you'll find its sham,
Where whimsy and wisdom unite.

The Silent Sentinel's Watch

In the park where critters play,
Stands a tree that can't sway.
With branches wide, it holds the sky,
Puffing up like it's shy.

Squirrels scamper up its trunk,
While birds chirp and sing in funk.
Its bark, a wrinkled frown of glee,
Cracks a joke—Oh, do you see?

A raccoon appears with a hat,
Thinking it's quite a cool cat.
The tree just chuckles, leaves a-ruffle,
"You've got to find the right shuffle!"

Underneath, the kids all laugh,
Creating shadows, a silly craft.
"Oh mighty tree!" they shout so loud,
"Do you have a secret crowd?"

Arbor Vitae Tales

Once a seed with dreams so bright,
Sprouted up to steal the light.
"I'll be tall!" it declared with glee,
"Just you wait and watch, you'll see!"

Bugs crawled up, in quite a fuss,
"Who invited you?" "Not us!"
With a laugh, it swayed so proud,
Flaunting leaves before the crowd.

"Hey, Mr. Wind, let's have some fun!
Twist and twirl until we're done!"
But on a gust, it flipped right round,
"Whoa, hold tight! I'm off the ground!"

And when it rains, it shouts with glee,
"Splash dance, everyone, come see me!"
So next time when in wooded trails,
Remember these tall, funny tales.

Whispers to the Wind

A breeze tickles through the leaves,
"Hey there, squirrel, time to weave!"
The branches sway, a silly dance,
While sunbeams play a golden trance.

"Oh Wind," the tree begins to tease,
"Don't mess my hair, if you please!"
But off it goes, a playful gust,
And leaves it looking quite robust.

Chattering birds join in the fun,
"A race with clouds, oh this'll be done!"
With laughter echoing in the air,
The tree shimmies, without a care.

So if you hear the branches creak,
It's giggles shared, not secrets bleak.
Join the choir of rustling cheer,
Where nature's jokes are always near.

Threads of Nature's Legacy

In the heart of a leafy glade,
A tree makes jokes about its shade.
"Try to hide? Too late, my friend!
Under my limbs, on me you depend!"

Creatures gather, tales unfold,
Every ring tells of fun, bold.
"Did you see that owl's wild dance?
It missed its perch—what was his chance?"

A wise old crow shakes its head,
"Life's a joke!" it caws instead.
"With every turn, and every leaf,
We weave our story, no grief!"

From the past, the laughter trails,
Through stories spun like nature's sails.
And in this grove of giggles bright,
Life's threads shimmer with pure delight.

Ancestral Voices of the Forest

In the woods where squirrels chatter,
Old trees gossip with a clatter.
They share tales with the breeze,
Of acorns lost and rusty keys.

Roots laugh as worms wiggle dance,
While branches wave in a prance.
The leaves whisper jokes in green,
Where even the bark's quite keen.

A raccoon peeks from a knot,
And says, "Ever heard of a spot?"
The forest echoes their delight,
As stars twinkle in the night.

And in this jolly canopy,
Fungi tease with a sense of glee.
Who knew that trees could jest so?
Nature's humor steals the show.

The Legacy of Timeless Watchers

Timeless guardians high and stout,
With branches wide, they twist about.
They've seen things that make you chuckle,
Like owls caught in a silly shuffle.

Their trunks bear scars of windy fights,
As critters play under moonlit nights.
Bees buzz in a chorus bold,
While acorns drop like tales retold.

Each ring within tells a jest,
Of seasons passed with funky fest.
The tree frogs croak in perfect tune,
Sharing puns beneath the moon.

From roots that tickle to crowns that sway,
Nature's laughter lights the way.
Inside this forest, joy springs high,
With every wink from the sky.

Dreams Cradled in Canopies

Beneath the leaves, dreams do play,
In sun-drenched spots, they laugh all day.
Squirrels hide their secret schemes,
While sunlight beams on leafy dreams.

Chipmunks chatter, sharing pride,
As shadows dance on nature's slide.
A jumping bug sings out loud,
In this silly, leafy crowd.

The sky plays games with twinkling lights,
As beetles plan their late-night flights.
Branches sway with giggling cheer,
While dreaming creatures draw near.

In this cozy, green embrace,
Life's a jumble, a joyous race.
Every whisper, every tease,
In dreams woven through the trees.

Echoes in the Embrace of Earth

When roots grow deep and laughter flows,
You'll find where nature's humor grows.
Through earthy hugs and leafy shout,
The forest plays games, there's no doubt.

Rabbits giggle at fallen leaves,
While dirt piles narrate the thieves.
Each grain of soil holds a tale,
Of wiggly worms that never fail.

In shadows thick, the laughter hums,
As rabbits bounce and the groundhog drums.
A raccoon's prank lights up the ground,
Echoes of joy all around.

Among the whispers of gentle streams,
Are pastel dreams of sunlit beams.
While roots embrace and branches twirl,
Nature's joy unfurls in a whirl.

The Wisdom of Falling Leaves

Leaves tremble in a breezy spin,
Dancing down with a cheeky grin.
They whisper tales of autumn's jest,
Making trees feel like second-best.

A squirrel laughs as he dives below,
Collecting treasures for winter's show.
"Why stay rigid?" he scoffs, full of cheer,
"Spread your colors, then disappear!"

The branches wave as if to wave,
"Let's party hard, be bold, be brave!"
Yet when the ground takes them with glee,
They shout, "At least we're wild and free!"

The earth embraces every fall,
Gathering giggles, a leafy ball.
In the end, they know it's true,
Life's just a dance in this funny view.

Requiem for the Aging Giants

Once proud sentinels, tall and spry,
Now sporting wrinkles, reaching for sky.
They chuckle low, like old pals do,
"Remember when our branches broke through?"

Beneath their bark, wisdom they store,
They moan, "The ache of growing lore!"
Yet each creak brings a laugh, a tease,
"Who knew age could be such a breeze?"

The acorns drop with a plop and a thud,
"We too have had our share of mud!"
As each limb quivers in the wind,
They hold their history, like old friends pinned.

"Fallen leaves tell tales of our past,
Of storms we've weathered, bold and steadfast.
So let's embrace this aging grace,
And dance to time's ridiculous pace!"

Songs of Soil and Sky

Underneath the surface, roots do hum,
"Hey there, sky!" they call, "We're not so glum!"
While clouds float by, the roots all sing,
"Got any rain? We're thirsty, bling!"

The sun pokes fun, "You're down so low,
But without you, where would we grow?"
The soil replies with a hearty clap,
"Together we make the world a map!"

"Let's share some secrets," they grin and plot,
As saplings listen in, curious a lot.
They giggle as the breeze sweeps by,
"A chat with clouds, oh my, oh my!"

With laughter swirling in nature's dance,
Each drop of rain a silly chance.
In songs of soil, in songs of sky,
They find the joy where the funny bits lie.

From Seedling to Sentinel

Tiny seedling with dreams so grand,
Wonders if it can take a stand.
"I'll stand so tall, a giant I'll be,
Just wait and see!" it chirps with glee.

Years rumble by, a trunk so strong,
But echoes of youth hum a playful song.
The wind cracks jokes about old tree bark,
"Remember when you were just a spark?"

Branches stretch, a leafy arm wave,
"Growing up here is like being brave!
From acorn dreams to mighty heights,
Life's a circus, full of delights!"

As sunset brews, leaves start to cheer,
"I'm fabulous now, oh how I steer!
From tiny dreams to a guardian watch,
Let's celebrate growth, it's quite the hatch!"

Branches in the Breeze

Branches dance with glee,
Whispering secrets of the sea.
Squirrels chase, they never tire,
As leaves applaud, they never expire.

Breezes tickle, branches sway,
Birds on high join in the play.
Raccoons giggle in the night,
As shadows play in soft moonlight.

Conversations with the Celestial Canopy

Stars peek through the leafy haze,
And giggle softly at our ways.
Moonbeams chuckle, twinkling bright,
As I argue with a firefly's flight.

Having chats with breezy friends,
Where laughter never seems to end.
Clouds pass by, with dreamy sighs,
They join the fun under starry skies.

A Heritage of Roots

Roots deep down in playful jest,
Holding stories of the best.
Worms do waltzes, quite absurd,
While ants have tea and sing a word.

Legends whispered through the bark,
As critters gather 'round at dark.
Each twist and turn, a tale they weave,
Of all the laughter that they believe.

Seasons of Swaying Shadows

Springtime giggles, buds appear,
Flowers bloom, bring cheer near.
Bees buzz along, what a sound,
In nature's dance, joy is found.

Summer's warmth, the branches sway,
Sunny days invite the play.
Pine cones rolling, oh what fun,
Who knew shadows could run?

Life Amongst the Leafy Giants

In the shade we play and laugh,
Squirrels dance, a ballet staff.
Chasing shadows, dodging beams,
Ticklish grass and sunny dreams.

A wise old tree gives sage advice,
"Don't touch my bark, it's not so nice!"
But we climb high, like monkeys free,
Swinging down, oh joyous spree!

Birds gossip from their lofty peaks,
Sharing tales of fun and squeaks.
A raccoon joins, he's quite the clown,
Hiding snacks, then tumbling down!

As daylight fades, we chase the sun,
Under leaves, we're still not done.
In this forest, joy feels vast,
Our laughter echoes, here we last.

Whispers in the Canopy

Up above, the leaves do chatter,
Saying things that make me splatter!
A squirrel's tale as wild as rain,
"Did you hear? A frog's a train!"

Branches sway to tune of jest,
"Who's the funniest?" they jest.
The sun peeks in, like a cheeky kid,
Winking at secrets that we hid.

A sloth sits slow with wise old eyes,
While ants parade with tiny pies.
"I'll take a bite!" the crow then shouts,
But ants scream loud, "We have no doubts!"

In the evening wrap, shadows play,
Giggles dance along the way.
In the canopy, laughter gleams,
Life's a joke, woven with dreams.

Beneath the Ancient Boughs

Underneath these mighty trees,
I hear a tale on the breeze.
A bear that wanted just to spin,
But tripped and fell into a bin!

The branches gave a hearty shake,
Laughing at how the bear's mistakes.
A funny sight, so round and stout,
"I didn't mean to!" he gave a shout.

Beneath the boughs, frogs start to croak,
Sharing puns of goofy folk.
A lizard glides with stylish flair,
Saying, "Wise guys don't wear hair!"

The sun dips low, our fun's not done,
With critters laughing, everyone.
In this hall of laughter's glow,
Beneath these giants, joy does flow.

A Symphony of Leaves

Leaves rustle like a funny band,
Drumming softly, nature's hand.
A caterpillar with a sax,
Plays smooth tunes, no time to relax!

Bees buzz round like busy friends,
Dancing high, where the laughter bends.
The grasshoppers join with their own flair,
Tapping feet, without a care.

A fox prances, takes a bow,
While the owl giggles, "Look at him now!"
Together they spin, a wild show,
Nature's antics, forever in flow.

Underneath this leafy dome,
We find laughter, we find home.
In this symphony, joy's our theme,
Life's a concert, forever a dream.

Echoes of Eternity

In the woods where whispers play,
Branches chat in a quirky way.
Squirrels giggle, dancing free,
Sharing tales of who made the tree.

Leaves rustle with a hearty cheer,
"Hey, you acorn, come lend an ear!"
Roots stretch deep, but they remain,
Laughing at the weather's claim.

Breezes carry secrets wide,
As nature's jesters take their ride.
Echoing laughter, on and on,
The party starts, then it's all gone.

Every branch a story spun,
In this forest, there's so much fun.
With every ring a joke unfolds,
A merry heart in wood that holds.

The Melody of Sturdy Roots

Beneath the ground, a band does jam,
Roots strumming tunes, oh what a scam!
Nutty rodents lend their voice,
All join in, quite by choice.

From cracks and crevices, beats arise,
Mice tap-dance, to everyone's surprise.
The ground shakes with laughter's sound,
A rhythm that can shake the ground.

A raccoon taps with a nimble paw,
While frogs croak in awe of the draw.
The saplings sway, caught in the groove,
Nature's dance, a silly move.

Here's to the roots, those merry brutes,
Strumming tunes in our funny boots!
In this garden, joy takes flight,
With every note, the world feels right.

Silent Witness of Generations

Standing tall, a grin so wide,
Branching out with joyful pride.
"Look at them growing, aren't they sweet?"
As squirrels gather for tasty treats.

Through storm and sun, it nods and sways,
Charting the years in chuckles and plays.
Ancestors whisper from leaves above,
Spreading wisdom, laughter, and love.

The trunk holds secrets, layers so sly,
Of clumsy climbers and a strange pie.
Every ring a giggle or two,
Echoing jokes shared between the crew.

As seasons change, it watches the dance,
Nature's antics, a merry romance.
With each new sprout, it starts to grin,
A funny reminder of where we've been.

Portraits of the Wild Expanse

In the wild, where laughter roams,
Woodpeckers paint with their funny homes.
A canvas of branches, leaves, and glee,
Creating art, wild and free.

Creatures pose for a cheeky snap,
Otters diving, avoiding a trap.
Every glance a quirky scene,
In this gallery where all are keen.

With rabbit ears and raccoon eyes,
Each frame filled with playful surprise.
Nature's selfies, wild and free,
Captured moments, just wait and see.

Through the brush, wild portraits pass,
Every creature wears a funny sash.
In this vast expanse, laughter thrives,
Every snapshot keeps joy alive.

Tales of Timber and Time

In the forest deep and wide,
Trees hold secrets, none can hide.
A squirrel juggles acorns neat,
While a rabbit taps his funny feet.

Leaves play hide and seek in breeze,
Making shadows dance with ease.
A woodpecker drums a silly tune,
While raccoons plot under the moon.

Branches wiggle as if to tease,
Grasshoppers leap with utmost ease.
A tree stump joins in with a grin,
Saying, "Let the wild games begin!"

With laughter echoing through the glade,
Nature's merriment is displayed.
In this green world, joy resides,
Where every creature playfully confides.

A Tapestry of Seasons

Springtime giggles, flowers sway,
Bumblebees buzz in a frolic play.
Summer sun has a silly grin,
As ants march on with chubby kin.

Autumn drops leaves, they whirl and twirl,
While squirrels plot their acorn pearl.
Winter whispers jokes from frosty air,
Snowmen chuckle, without a care.

Each season wears a capricious face,
Telling tales in a wild embrace.
Watch the magic, it's all in fun,
Nature's canvas, second to none!

As day meets night, they swap their rhyme,
Winking stars join in the time.
With every shift and playful twist,
A tapestry of joy you can't resist!

The Silent Watcher

In the glen, a giant stands,
Whispering secrets with ancient hands.
He's seen it all from dawn to dusk,
From silly pranks to leaves' bright husk.

Birds gather round to share a laugh,
As he listens to their silly gaff.
A turtle slips on a mossy stone,
While frogs join in, a ribbit zone!

With roots that stretch, he's quite the seer,
Witnessing antics year after year.
He chuckles low, a gentle sound,
As mischief blooms all around.

Though standing tall and ever still,
He guards each giggle, each tiny thrill.
A sentinel of laughter, timeless yet spry,
In the heart of the forest, the silent eye.

Vestiges of Verdant Wisdom

Amidst the green, the wise ones gaze,
With beards of moss, they catch the rays.
Old stumps recall the laughter past,
While shadows of fun are unsurpassed.

"Why did the tree cross the glade?"
To have a laugh with friends in shade!
Laughter echoes, round and round,
Among the leaves, it's all profound.

Wisdom's roots run deep and wide,
In every giggle, stories reside.
An acorn's dream of sprouting tall,
Comes wrapped in laughter, never small.

So come and join this merry dance,
In nature's arms, take a chance.
For in every leaf and branch's sway,
Is laughter living day by day.

Tales Etched in Twigs

In a forest so charming, a twig took a stroll,
Thinking it could dance, oh what a goal!
Frogs laughed and ribbited, 'You think you can groove?'
But the twig tripped, and the toads went 'Whoa, dude!'

Squirrels on branches rolled eyes in delight,
As the twig spun around, an incredible sight!
A leaf dropped in laughter, 'You can't steal the show!'
But the twig, in its pride, yelled, 'Watch me, oh no!'

Beetles in bowties brought snacks for the fun,
While the twig told tall tales of the races it won.
Everyone chuckled, some even brought drinks,
And soon the whole forest was drawn into sync!

So remember this tale of the twirling old limb,
In the heart of the woods, where laughter is brim.
Who needs a grand stage or a plump, plucky star?
When a twig can incite joy, you've truly gone far!

Seasons of the Majestic Sentinel

When autumn arrived, the leaves dressed in cheer,
They cloaked themselves golden, then whispered, 'Oh dear!'
The wind gusted gently, a leaf took a dive,
Screaming, 'I'm flying!' like it had to survive!

Winter slapped snow on the branches so grand,
The squirrels built snowmen, the best in the land.
They added a scarf made of twigs and a hat,
While the trees chuckled softly, 'Now that's an idea!'

Spring brought the blossoms with colors so bright,
Yet bees were confused, buzzing left, then right.
'Where's the honey?' they buzzed, 'Is it here or it's there?'
But flowers just giggled, 'Ah, bees, we don't care!'

In summer, the sun cast a playful warm ray,
As the trees turned to shade, inviting kids to play.
They swung from the branches and giggled with glee,
In the theater of nature, joy flowed free!

The Stillness of Verdant Watchers

In the quiet of night, the trees shared a joke,
'Why did the squirrel bring a ladder to smoke?'
'He wanted to reach just the top of the tree!'
The owls hooted laughter, 'Oh dear, can it be?'

With branches entwined, they passed tales around,
Of acorns with attitudes and nuts that got crowned.
'Then came the raccoons with their masks all askew,
Declaring, 'No snacks for the deer; they're too few!'

A sloth hung nearby, with a grin on his face,
Saying, 'Life is a race, but I'm winning this space!'
But the trees just nodded, 'Slow is the way,
In the calm of the night, enjoy every sway.'

So these watchers stand guard, with humor to share,
In the stillness of night, there's laughter in air.
Whispers of nature, where crickets will chirp,
And the stories stay safe from the sneaky night burp!

Cradle of the Forest Spirits

In a cradle of branches, where spirits entwine,
Lay a quirky old gnome, sipping sweet pine wine.
He said with a grin, 'I've seen better days,
ut who needs a crown when you've got such good rays?'

The fairies danced circles, their twinkles aglow,
Mistaking the gnome for a celebrity show.
They cooed, 'Oh dear friend, come join us in flight!'
He waved with a laugh, 'Just don't be too bright!'

The mushrooms all chuckled at their lively chat,
'You should see the deer getting stuck in their hat!'
Said a wise old owl, perched high on a twig,
'Watch out for that gnome, he'll dance a fat jig!'

So laughter adorned this woodland retreat,
Where spirits and creatures made joy quite complete.
In the cradle of leaves, with stories unfurled,
A funny old gnome ruled his whimsical world!

Tales from the Heartwood

Once a squirrel thought he could fly,
Wore acorn hats as he zipped by.
Up in the branches, he spun with glee,
Until he crashed right into a tree!

A wise old crow cawed from above,
"Flying's not easy, my feathery dove!"
The squirrel laughed, shook off the dirt,
Said, "Next time, I'll try without the skirt!"

Raccoon on a racetrack made of twigs,
Claimed he was racing with lightning digs.
But all he did was trip on his tail,
And rolled right down, oh, how he did wail!

In the shadows, laughter would ring,
As critters debated who'd fly or swing.
They argued with jest, from far and near,
In a forest of giggles, both loud and clear.

Fragments of the Timbered Past

Back in the day, when the trunks were spry,
The trees knew secrets that made them sigh.
Bark tales spun by each year's tough ring,
About the time they became a swing!

Fungi held parties, mushrooms in hats,
Dancing beneath an old willow's chats.
"Who's got the fruit punch?" one shouted with glee,
Only to find moldy logs sipping tea!

A badger once claimed he could outsmart the sun,
But ended up hiding from everyone.
He thought he could beat twilight's embrace,
Yet stumbled home, lost in his own race!

The breeze carried tales from winters past,
Whispering laughter, oh how it laughed!
Each knot and notch held a story or two,
Of the funny things trees sometimes knew.

Blessings in Every Leaf Drop

Leaves danced down in a fluttery cheer,
Each drop a blessing, or so they would cheer.
Hopscotching critters caught in mid-air,
With branchy choreography laid out with care.

A shy little chipmunk, clumsy and neat,
Wore a leaf crown on his fuzzy head fleet.
He strutted about, feeling quite grand,
Till the wind swirled his crown from his hand!

Raindrops tickled, in a humorous way,
As the saplings giggled through a cloudy day.
"Why can't we play?" one tiny sprout cried,
The raindrops just splashed, "We'll be your guide!"

So in each leaf, while it danced on the breeze,
Was laughter and joy, a forest tease.
With every plop on the ground from above,
They spread giggles and tales, oh so full of love!

The Call of the Wind-Born Seeds

Seeds drifting down like a feathered jest,
Spun in the wind on their holiday quest.
One boldly yelled, "I'm off to see light!"
Yet tangled in branches, he lost his flight!

Another had dreams of growing quite tall,
But landed smack dab by a squirrel's small hall.
"Stay for a snack!" beckoned the tiny host,
As the seed pondered if this was a roast.

Traveling buddies with stories to share,
Planted their hopes, knowing life's never fair.
For each gust of wind that whirled them around,
Brought laughter and chaos, oh what a sound!

So the seeds laughed as they took to the air,
Carried away on nature's wild flair.
No need for a map or a guidebook to see,
Life's an adventure, just droppin' a seed!

Guardians of the Timeworn Grove

In the grove where squirrels dance,
Old trees tell tales of chance,
Acorns roll with silly grace,
Nature's jesters, a wild race.

Winds whisper secrets up so high,
While chipmunks plot with mischief sly,
Branches sway, a chuckling crew,
As dandelions join the view.

With mushrooms wearing tiny hats,
And raccoons sneaking snacks like brats,
The elder trees just shake their leaves,
At all the chaos nature weaves.

From roots to limbs, they play their part,
Guardians of the woodsy art,
Laughter echoes, sweetly bold,
In this haven, life unfolds.

Echoes of the Woodland Heart

In twilight's glow, the woods ignite,
With owls who hoot in pure delight,
The rhythm of the nighttime choir,
Sings echoes, quirks that never tire.

Slugs wear coats of sparkling dew,
As crickets sing their songs, so true,
The woodland heart, a quirky beat,
For every creature in retreat.

Mice sip tea from acorn cups,
While beetles organize their ups,
Beneath the stars, the forest pranks,
United voices, all the ranks.

This symphony, a playful show,
As nature laughs and dances slow,
In every leaf, a story spun,
The woodland heart, forever fun.

Memories Carved in Bark

In every tree a story lives,
Each ring a laugh that nature gives,
Bark adorned with carvings bright,
Whimsical tales of day and night.

Squirrels' doodles, hearts entwined,
And raccoons drawing maps, designed,
They plot their escapades so grand,
With every scratch, a playful hand.

Woodpeckers drum like bands on stage,
While fireflies flicker, setting rage,
Of laughter shared amidst the leaves,
Where cherished memories never leave.

From roots to crown, a legacy,
Nature's scrapbook, wild and free,
In every bark, a chuckle found,
The forest's joy, unbound and sound.

Guardians of the Golden Acorn

Beneath the boughs where secrets lie,
Guardians, each with watchful eye,
Golden acorns shine, a prize,
For those who hop and scurry by.

Chipmunks claim their rightful share,
While hedgehogs flaunt their prickly flair,
The merry chase ignites the day,
In woodland games, they laugh and play.

The wise old owl, a judge esteemed,
Sees how the acorn dreams are schemed,
And under twinkling starlit skies,
The forest bursts with joyful cries.

Each acorn, like a treasure trove,
Holds silly moments to reproach,
In this wild realm of funny fate,
Guardians gather 'round, first-rate!

www.ingramcontent.com/pod-product-compliance
Lightning Source LLC
Chambersburg PA
CBHW071846160426
43209CB00003B/431